It was early in the morning when Mike and I drove through the huge stone gates of Yellowstone National Park. Though it was midsummer, the air was crisp and sunshine sparkled on the morning dew. We arrived early so we could find a place to camp. It was peak tourist season, and we had heard that all the campgrounds would be full by noon. I never understood why Yellowstone was so popular, but I was soon to find out.

After claiming one of the remaining campsites, we sat down and looked at the map of Yellowstone. The park is huge. It covers the northwestern corner of Wyoming, with portions extending into Idaho and Montana. Even if we had the whole summer, we could never explore the entire park. We circled the areas that looked the most interesting. The nearest attraction was just down the road. We climbed back in the car and headed toward Mammoth Hot Springs.

By now, many tourists were out and about. Each year, about 3 million people visit Yellowstone National Park. It seemed as though they all picked the same week as we did. Although we were driving, we moved slower than the pedestrians.

People swarmed about like ants at a picnic. Young kids ran wild despite the frantic pleas of their parents.

After several laps around the parking lot, we finally found an empty stall. We strolled the wooden walkways that lead to the springs, picking our way through other tourists. The raised platforms were built to protect both the visitors and the environment. In many areas of Yellowstone, the ground is thin and crusty. Boiling water lies just below the surface. Each year, a tourist or two who leaves the walkway breaks through to the boiling water below.

Why is there boiling water beneath the ground in Yellowstone? Earth is not a hard, solid rock like it appears from the surface. Deep inside the planet, the temperature is extremely hot. It is so hot that rocks melt into a thick, gooey substance called *magma*. In most places, magma is many miles beneath the ground. In Yellowstone, it is much closer to the surface. If you touch the ground, you can feel the heat. The warm rocks heat water that sinks into the ground, making Yellowstone a land of hot springs and steam.

As we walked, the platform creaked and groaned under our weight. It seemed to be calling for our attention. The only thing I could pay attention to was the colorful, musical water and thick, billowing steam. The water gushed out of the ground and spilled over layered waterfalls.

pick up speed and carve deeper into the earth. We crossed the river and parked the car. When we opened the doors, we heard what sounded like the roar of thunder, but the sky was clear. We saw the source of the noise after a short hike through the woods. The Yellowstone River plummeted over a cliff and crashed to the bottom of a canyon. As far as we could see, steep rock walls towered above the river.

As the sun sunk toward the canyon rim, we headed back to our campsite. Along the way, we often saw groups of people out of their cars and crouched in the weeds. Our minds searched for an explanation. We finally stopped to see what the commotion was. Peering into some nearby trees, we spotted a herd of bison. At later stops, we saw elk, moose, and mule deer. The animals in Yellowstone are protected from hunters. It is one of the few places in America where large animal herds still roam.

The next morning, we paid a visit to Old Faithful, Yellowstone's most famous landmark. Old Faithful is a *geyser*, one of 200 scattered across the park's basins. Geysers are curious folk. They are hot springs that thrust water and steam into the air. Each geyser has its unique personality. The most powerful geysers thrust water hundreds of feet above the ground. Some eruptions last only a few minutes, while others last for hours. Many geysers are so irregular that it's impossible to guess when they will erupt next. Old Faithful,

on the other hand, erupts about once every hour. It has not missed an eruption during the past 100 years.

We arrived at Old Faithful at just the right time. As we sat down among the other tourists, the geyser blew. Forceful spurts of water spewed high into the air and crashed back to the ground. Puffs of steam billowed upward. Grandparents gasped, children squealed, and teenagers observed the spectacle in silence. We laughed. Old Faithful looked like nature's own water fountain.

After watching Old Faithful erupt, we decided to hike up a trail that promised a unique view of the famous geyser. The trail began at an area bubbling with activity. The first attraction was a *fumarole*—essentially a geyser without water. When a fumarole erupts, all that escapes is steam. The fumarole in front of us looked as if it were the earth's mouth. It belched just as we approached. Puffs of gray steam billowed out of the ground as the smell of rotten eggs floated into my nose. We watched, our jaws open in awe, until the smell began to bother us—which was longer than you may think!

To me, the most interesting attractions were the hot springs. Each spring looks, smells, and sounds unlike any other. Some look evil and wicked, like a witch's brew of poison. Others look like pots of boiling water, clean and clear. Some are dull gray or sickly yellow, while others are

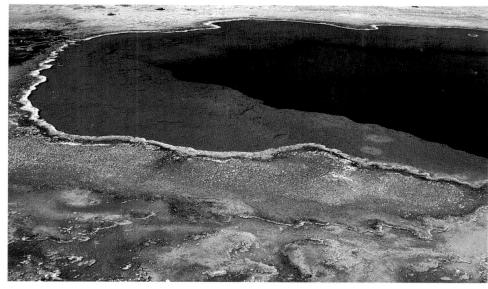

outlined with brilliant yellows, greens, and blues. Some springs have water bubbling and splashing over their edges like over-filled swimming pools. Other springs, lacking water, look like pots of colorful, bubbling mud.

We sweated in the hot sun as we headed up the trail. Scattered alongside the trail were groves of burnt trees, reminders of the fire of 1988. The tree trunks were pitch-black, but many limbs were white—apparently spared from the scorching flames. In places, gleeful clumps of flowers covered the ground, adding color to the desolate scene.

We reached the overlook after a long uphill climb. We peered out across the valley. Scattered here and there, clouds of steam rose in the air. Old Faithful was easy to pick out—its steam rose higher than all the rest. We sat for a while, watching the steam below and the weather above. The sky was preparing for its afternoon storm. After the cloudburst the day before, we were familiar with these sudden storms. This time we were prepared with rain ponchos.

The rain started lightly, but quickly grew in intensity. The trail turned to mud. We trudged along, bombed by heavy raindrops but happy to be under our ponchos. White streaks of lightning flashed through the gray clouds. Thunder bellowed. Then, quite suddenly, hail began to pelt us and the ground. The hailstones were smaller

than peas, so they tickled more than they hurt! Then, off in the distance, a patch of blue sky peeked into view. We hid beneath a tree and waited for the sun to return. With smiles on our faces, we squished and squashed our way back to the car.

That night, staring at the star-filled sky, I realized why so many people flock to Yellowstone. Most of us live our lives as a routine. The sun rises, we go about our daily chores, and we return to our heated houses and favorite television shows. Away from our artificial cities and daily routines, nature is waiting to startle us with a geyser, a herd of bison, or a hailstorm. In Yellowstone, there is another surprise at every turn.

THE CHILD'S WORLD
NATUREBOOKS

Wildlife Library

Alligators

Arctic Foxes

Bald Eagles

Beavers

Birds

Black Widows

Camels

Cheetahs

Coyotes

Dogs

Dolphins

Elephants

Fish

Giraffes

Insects

Kangaroos

Lions

Mammals

Monarchs

Musk-oxen

Octopuses

Owls

Penguins

Polar Bears

Primates

Rattlesnakes

Reptiles

Rhinoceroses

Seals and Sea Lions

Sharks

Snakes

Spiders

Tigers

Walruses

Whales

Wildcats

Wolves

Zebras

Space Library

Earth

Mars

The Moon

The Sun

Adventure Library

Glacier National Park

The Grand Canyon

Yosemite

Yellowstone National Park